Learn the *Secrets* of Studying at U.S. Colleges and Universities

Nigel G. Williamson

A Step by Step Guide to study at a US College or University

Learn the Secrets of Studying At a US College: A Step-by-step guide for International Students

Nigel G. Williamson

www.rekindlemylife.com

Table of Contents

Dedication

*This book is dedicated to my wife Shonette Althea
and sons Sharlon, Jamal, Jayden, Jelani and Joel*

Acknowledgement

I want to thank God for this vision, my kids for putting
summer on
hold as I pen a second book and for my wife too for all the
time, faith and dedication as I sit in the loft.
I want to thank the Reaching UP Show Team.
Cherry Sorzano, my associate producer for keeping
me on track when I don't know which way to turn.
Claudette Haynes my friend and partner who encouraged
me and work with me on crunching the numbers and
on making this show a weekly dream come through.
Mussie, Yared, David, Noah, Sara, Lettie,
and all the other people at EBS TV who watch me and
guide me each week as I present to 25 million viewers
hope,
purpose and a dream to live a better life.

My personal journey in a few words…

When I first arrived into the US, I was told that nothing is possible. In fact, coming to the US was the first part of an impossible feat becoming possible. At the time, I worked for a youth program and was offered training and I choose to attend. Then I was offered a scholarship and like many, my response was simple, I cannot go to school since I don't have the money, I was shown a scholarship, I applied and then I was approved.

After a series of events, my uncle decided I will no longer attend that school, he wanted me to live here in Maryland with him, I was upset, the scholarship at Hood College was great, I know I saw it said $20,000 so I needed to get that money but the location was far from where I would stay and without a lot of money, it would be difficult.

It was then that I was told the unthinkable, "go get a student loan and I will sign it!" I eagerly went to work on finding a loan and each and every one I asked, told me I cannot get one. I went reading books, researching the internet and would even sit down in book stores, pouring over books on scholarships until one day I stumbled upon one in a book store in Washington, DC; I know I had found my dream. I quickly call the place, get the information and was able to secure a loan for college. Coupled with my scholarship, I was able to get my dreams achieved and today, I have a US college degree and I am finishing a British Masters.

We live in a world where our dreams can be easily dashed, like me, I want you all to know that no matter how high your dreams may be, and you can find the resources to make them come through. It's your determination, perseverance and dedication that will determine the outcome.

*Some years ago, I received a call from Ms. Betty Taylor, (a woman from my church) very late at night asking me about the organization that helped me get my loan. I told her, she was desperate to help her son get funding for school and being an international student, he too was finding the maze frustrating. After giving them the information, I started talking with my wife about the constant frustrations many students face who do not know where to turn for resources. Her suggestions are what you hold in your hands. **A road map for students to understand and succeed in US colleges and Universities.***

Privately, I was working with a select few students and I was building a little name through Reaching UP and Youth Connex, both were my organizations and I was not prepared to take on more.

But the constant calls and emails were getting the best of me and I had to make a decision. I don't tell people about my scholarship course at www.rekindlemylife.com unless they know me. It's not that I am selfish, but I did not want to stretch my team more. We currently get request from all around the world and I wrote this book is a teachable fashion to provide that bridge for those looking for a guide. When I did the mid-season series on International Students on the Reaching UP show, everything changed, everyone started calling, and everyone found me.

6

*So in a few words, you have my journey, my purpose And a guide. Take some time to learn it. As I say each week on Reaching Up Show, it's possible to....**know better**, **do better** and ultimately **LIVE BETTER-Nigel***

part one

Introduction

1. Where it all started?

"Each year, 500,000 students leave their home country and journey to colleges and universities in the United States for a chance at making themselves better as International Students. Only 10% will succeed at completing college in 4 years, 15% will run out of cash in their first year and 30% will quit school and settle for low paying jobs."

These figures are real and often are never given emphasis in your home country since many do not know this happens. While some are fortunate to enjoy the luxuries of wealthy family and scholarships and even a mentor to help them along, the sad truth is MOST don't. They leave their homeland and enter the maze to be quickly consumed by the jungle called 'International Student Syndrome'. After running out of cash, making poor choices and stumbling over again and again, they ended up frustrated, many quit school and others head back home broken hearted.

The burden of college for many has left them not seeking options to become better or to avoid seeking a solution for their educational dreams. While education provides options for many, the international students are limited by just the choices in funding, schooling, scholarships and "how-to".

Secondly, once you start the journey of the international student, not knowing the 'how to do things' can be a challenge. This guide will give you starting the tools you need to become a successful student in the US and some knowledge to navigate the international student maze.

Lastly, I write this book to deal with the first set of information you can have and to provide some direction on starting this journey today. Not because I have a desire to sound important but because I have seen enough people who get trapped into the maze and also because I too had to learn the challenges as I too was an international student, made those mistakes and learn a lot of painful lessons.

The New Trends

Our world is emerging, things that once were only for just a select few, are now accessible to all, the era has change from one of power, wealth and dominance to one of information, change and significance. People are finding out this the hard way. Recently, I interviewed the International Student Advisor for Howard University in Washington, DC for my show that airs in Ethiopia, within a few days; he was inundated with email and phone calls from people from around the world. That one 30 minutes interview was so impacting, that people the world over were asking for information, tools and help to come to school in the USA. That was a major reason, I wrote this book.

My second reason came after my team did a pilot on survey on Facebook; we ask people a simple question, **"Please help me to name my book?"**

The results were surprising, people is 35 countries got this information and entered their Names, Email addresses and some went on to asking for a course giving us their full Mailing Addresses, Phone number and they gave us the feedback we needed. They were highly in need of a program to guide them.

I could not simply resist the need to share with people the information since I was teaching people this process personally for the past 5-7years.

Over the last 10 years the number of students coming to America for higher studies have increased manifold. With liberalization and Internet revolution, even students of the middle-income families find it an extremely practical and affordable option. In spite of this, we have experienced that more students lose the opportunity of studying in the USA not because they cannot afford it but because they do not have accurate and relevant information about how to go about it.

My team has guiding students towards higher studies in the USA through our offices, internet articles, TV programs and online training. This book is also aimed at providing accurate guidance and up to date information about educational opportunities in the USA. We sincerely hope that the students and more particularly the parents will find information in this book very useful while planning careers. We once again state that students lose on to the opportunity of studying in the USA not because they cannot afford but because they do not have information about the possibility.

Peter was an average student with only average marks in Rwanda. However, he was keenly interested in pursuing certificate in aviation. He wanted to fly planes and this was not possible in his home country. After learning about the opportunities through Short

Programs in the USA, he was able to gain acceptance into a program in Florida, with a special accelerated program. He was successful also in gaining a full scholarship and was able to come to USA to study. He completed all the formalities in eighteen months and is now pursuing his dream career. He is fully certified as a private and commercial pilot in the USA. We feel happy for being of help to such students and we take pride in helping him build their careers.

Rowie was a brilliant student with a passion for environmental studies, with no degree offered in her home countries St. Vincent and the Grenadines; she set sight on pursuing studies in the US. With no internet access in her community, she started the research in her local library. Rowie was successful in finding scholarships all the way from her Associate Degree then for her Bachelor's Degree and later her Masters and Ph. D. Thinking that education in the US will be expensive, she was nervous about the whole process, but she was able to navigate the journey, find her passion and not only was she successful in finding funding for herself, but also for her husband who accompanied her who too is completing a fully funded Ph. D here in the US.

There are hundreds of students like **Peter** and **Rowie** who have gained from the information about study opportunities in the USA. You can also go through the various chapters in this book and understand all the pre requisites for studying in USA. If you need any further information, you are most welcome to visit our web site www.rekindlemylife.com.

part two

Why Study in the US?

2. Why Study in the USA?

The world has gotten smaller and communications can be submitted further and faster with today's technology. Globalization and Internet revolution has shrunk the world into a global village. Boundaries of the nations are only politically important now. For the trade, commerce and industry, the world has become one market place. In such times, we need to have global compatibility to survive and grow. We need to have exposure to the various cultures and business practices of various countries.

Advantages of studying in USA

Sometime ago, I wrote a report called 10 reasons to study in USA. A simple report with no intention of offering it to others, after editing and design, I was intrigued to ask friends to review the information and quickly started receiving thank you messages as I stress some of the advantages that were too simple to many but powerful in communicating the impact that a US education has.

One must understand the advantages that US offers as a place for higher studies before investing the time and money. Also, it is not just enough to decide to study in the US just because it is trendy. We are therefore putting forth the most distinct advantages offered by the US education system:

  ✓ **International Exposure:** more than 500,000 international students come to study every year in the United States from different countries. No other country in the world attracts so many international students. Naturally, the international exposure that you get while being a part of such a diverse students body is one of the most important advantages of studying in the United Sates.

- ✓ **Educational Infrastructure:** as you study higher and higher, you need educational infrastructure, which is as important as the quality of syllabus and quality of teachers. The standards that the schools have to maintain to keep their accreditation force them to recruit some of the best faculty members whose work has been renowned and praised by many.

- ✓ **Research in the Universities:** this is the most distinct advantage of American Education System. Unlike most other universities in the world, the universities in the USA are engaged in conducting life changing research work for the benefit of the industry and government of the USA and the world at large. These researches are conducted under the supervision of the college professors and the students get an opportunity to work on these research projects.

- ✓ **Career Choices:** with more than 5,000 universities and colleges offering tens of thousands of different programs, the choice of careers is the widest in the United States. There is nothing which is worth pursuing a career in which is not covered by the American higher education system.

- ✓ **Flexibility:** American education system is credit hour based. These credits are widely transferable from one university to another. Also, you can take credit hours as per your requirements and therefore the duration of completing a four-year degree may range from three to five years as per the capacity of the student.

- ✓ **Acceptability:** The ability not to face discrimination is a big factor in studying in the USA. How many times we come across a deserving student not getting a career of his choice? Dreams are often shattered because students lose their careers by a fraction of percentage and then they have no other choice but to either change their field of study or settle for an inferior institution in their home country. Such things rarely happen when you are applying to an American institution. The universities in the USA give due consideration to the desire of the students and admissions are based on a complete assessment of the students overall personality and not just the grades or transcripts.

Overall, the advantages of studying in America are far too many and most of the parents and students already know about them. But most of the time they are unaware about the affordability of the courses or the exact procedure and timetable for preparation. This book will deal with these issues in the subsequent chapters.

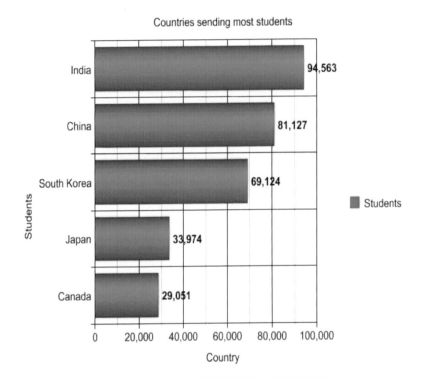

Countries sending most students

INTERNATIONAL EDUCATIONAL EXCHANGE

About 20% of the students studying in the USA are studying for a bachelor's degree. Most of the students are studying in fields such as engineering, information technology, core sciences and business management programs.

Also, if we compare the popularity of different countries amongst the students, once again, USA is on the top with substantial lead. A comparison of students in the major four countries of the world is "All the above statistics clearly indicates that international students have preferred USA as their most suitable destination for higher education abroad." This trend is likely to continue in future.

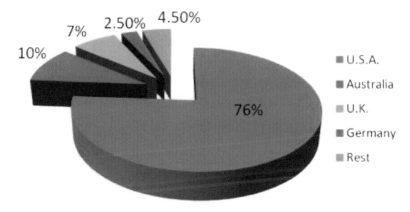

PERCENTAGE SHARE

International Students in Foreign Countries by Percentage

part three

About Reaching Up

3. About Reaching Up Show.

After successfully launching Youth Connex Show in 2007 that aired across the US in 25 cities providing guidance to Christian youth, I decided that it was time to shift my focus to many who are not this privilege. Youth Connex grew so fast and became so popular that I was pulled in every direction. When the show finally ended, I was simply tired, over worked and needed some rest. However, in the midst of this, I was given a call to help a new television station with a youth talk format. My goal was to share with people was to make a difference in their lives, how to find a positive future and to provide hope to many the world over. Reaching UP is tag line "Know Better: Do Better: Live Better" for that reason. The weekly upbeat talk format that airs across the East Africa, the Middle East and Europe has been gaining popularity. The amount of emails, friends comments on my fan page and likes and emails are a testament to the impact we are having and making on the people across the world.

Reaching UP Show is about making a positive impact; it's about sharing hope and giving people tools they can use today to make their lives better. This book is a part of the tools and resources we plan to make available to show people the path to higher education in the US. As I spend sleepless nights typing, I know that the show, the people and the resources will always be used by someone in some corner of the world. You can visit our website for more information visit http://www.reachingup.net for the latest information.

Vision and Mission of this project

Our vision is to provide a place with knowledge and tools are shared across the globe. As the world becomes a global village, we want to lead the charge giving people the opportunities to be equipped to lead careers, dreams and hope for a brighter future. Knowledge is power and those who Know better can do better and will ultimately Live better...

The mission of Reaching Up is to effectively share knowledge, guide careers, and help fulfill dreams of students around the world. To achieve this objective, Reaching Up has provided highly qualified and committed career counselors through a global infrastructure while making education and knowledge available to all.

Role of Reaching Up in personal development

Reaching Up has agreed to help 6,000 students this year to realize their dream of studying abroad. We have always believed in providing comprehensive services covering all aspects the process, be it academic, financial or administrative. Our highest contribution in the area of career development has come through the following achievements:

Middle Income Families: most of our students have come from middle-income families. Most of them always thought that studying abroad is unaffordable. However, our extensive research on the availability of scholarships and other funding opportunities have helped students of hundreds of families pursue their careers abroad.

Academic Performance: this is another area where Reaching Up has done substantial value addition in the careers of its students. While many education system is "high marks oriented, the American education system however, is much different. It gives importance to the OVERALL background of the student rather than his/ her grades alone. Reaching Up has utilized this feature of the system to the benefit of the students and even students

18

with average academic performance are studying the fields of their interests.

Our Team: Reaching UP has a team of highly qualified and motivated career counselors who are operating from its network of offices. Each one of them is experienced in guiding aspirations of the students and more importantly, they can draw knowledge from the experience of other team members. As a result, the most up to date and relevant information is available to the students. Also, you can visit the web site:

www.rekindlemylife.com

part four

Career Planning

4. Career Planning

As the choices of careers increase, the career planning becomes more and more important at the same time more and more complex. In such a situation, information is the key. If you have all the information, or know where to collect it from, your job is half done. The other half is to be in a position to analyze the information and make a decision. Reaching Up has been helping the students in collection as well as analysis of the information. This book is yet another initiative of Reaching Up to reach out to the students and parents to help them in their decision-making.

General objectives of students

At every milestone in the academic career of a student, he has to take a career decision. The choice of career you make at this stage determines your entire life ahead. Now, this choice of career is determined only when all the following factors exist simultaneously:

a) You are clear of what you want to do. (Field of Study)

b) You have all the information about the availability and acceptability criterions for this field in your home country and abroad.

c) Your academic performance is acceptable for admission into the field

d) Your family can afford to finance the education in the field

Now, let us look at each of these factors in greater detail to arrive at a proper decision:

a) Most of the students are clear on their major field of study. However, it is always a good idea to identify top three fields of your interest instead of just one. If you have a difficulty in making a choice, Reaching Up conducts aptitude tests to scientifically identify the fields that you are best suitable for.

b) Once you are clear of the field of study, start collecting information about where is it available, what is the condition of acceptability and what is the cost of education. This book will give you answers of these questions for opportunities in America. You can collect information for opportunities in your home country through various sources.

c) You can then take the relevant entrance tests for these courses conducted for different courses in your home country or USA (GRE, GMAT, SAT & TOEFL).

d) If your performance is acceptable in the entrance tests, you have to make arrangements for the funding of your career. But since you must have already collected information about the cost of education in stage a) above, you are already aware about the budget and so you start with your chosen career.

These steps may be simple to read, but we all know that there are so many factors, which make these simple looking steps extremely difficult at times. We therefore recommend that you be prepared for alternative plans if the main plan fails at any stage. This book is an effort to give you one such alternative.

Limitations of Education System

The most significant limitation of other country's education system is the uncertainty of admissions to certain select careers like sciences, engineering, medical etc. Even the most capable students are not assured of their seat in the desired college in spite of working hard for the entrance tests.

However, most students do not plan for this uncertainty in advance and as a result; they have to settle for career options, which were never their choice.

Every year we come across number of students who could not get through the entrance examinations or who are not enjoying their current jobs. They decide to pursue the option of studying in USA. In the whole process, they lose valuable time.

Who should plan to study in the USA?

We strongly recommend that the students and their parents should collect all the information about educational opportunities in America. If they find these opportunities suitable, they should take the GRE/ GMAT/ SAT & TOEFL tests one year before their intended arrival in USA. This will ensure that they get a career of their choice in America, immediately after their academic year is over.

Also, students who do not make it to the final list of selection of a course or a job their home country, should think of pursuing careers in the field of their interest in America rather than studying a subject, or taking a job, which is not of their interest in your home country.

Finally, the students who have made up their mind to study in America because they are convinced about the advantages that it offers, should complete the preparation in their last academic year in order to ensure that they don't lose time after their results.

part five

Cost of Education

5. Cost of Education

The cost of education is the most important Reaching Up or considered by almost every student from another country. Also, it's a wide spread belief that the education in USA is not affordable. The complicated structure of financing opportunities and the dynamics of scholarships, in campus and off campus jobs etc. make the financial planning further more difficult. At the outset, one may think that the cost of tuition plus the living expenses is equal to the total cost that a student requires. But then, what about scholarships? What about campus jobs? What about summer jobs? Will they reduce my total cost? To what extent? What is the certainty? This and many more variables make the financial planning process absolutely difficult at times.

We at Reaching UP, have been meticulously calculating the expected costs for different students. Our knowledge about the working methods of universities, local laws and quality consultation to the parents has helped many middle-income families comfortably manage the education of their children in America. While the cost factor has to be calculated separately for each student, we have given broad information about the various ingredients of costs as well as the funding opportunities in this chapter.

Tuition and Fees

US Universities fall under two major categories: public (state supported), and private (independent) institutions. International students' tuition expenses at state schools are based on nonresident costs, which are still usually less expensive than those of private universities. It's important to note that the cost of a program in a US school does not

24

necessarily affect its quality. Similarly, it is not a rule that all public universities are great or all private universities are inferior. One has to study each university independently, regardless of whether it is a public university or a private university.

The range of tuition fees charged by these universities is given below:

University Type	Average Tuition Fees (annual in U.S. Dollars)
Private Institutions (High Cost)	$ 25,000
Private Institutions (Low Cost)	$ 15,000
State Institutions (High Cost)	$ 20,000
State Institutions (Low Cost)	$ 10,000

The tuition fee is different for different universities and varies widely with courses. It can vary from as low as $ 7,000 a year for state universities to as much as $ 30000 a year for some private universities.

Living Expenses

The approximate annual living expenses are about $7,000, which includes accommodation as well as other daily expenses. However, the expenses are different for different people depending on the lifestyles and this is just a rough idea. The main expenses can be split up as:

Rent $ 400 per month

Groceries $ 100 per month

Utilities $ 100 per month

Phone $ 50 per month

Sundry $ 50 per month

So, about $700 per month is a good estimation. Most people can survive with $500- $600 a month. The key here is to share apartments/houses so that you save on the utilities, fixed charge portion of phone and to some extent on groceries

How to fund the cost of education

The total cost of tuition and living can be funded through the following sources:

- ✓ **Personal Savings:** this is the traditional method of funding education. Most parents meet the education expenses of their children through personal earnings and savings. But when it comes to financing the education in America, one should take care that the personal savings are utilized to the minimum possible extent. In some cases, we even recommend not to use personal savings at all to fund the education.

- ✓ **Educational Loans:** this is the new emerging option in the last couple of years. Many nationalized banks have a structured and uniform educational loan policy wherein loans are given to international students who have a co-signor or guarantee.

- ✓ **Scholarships:** Most American universities offer substantial scholarships to deserving students. These scholarships are given based on different

26

selection criterions. The next chapter is specifically dedicated for discussing the scholarships option.

- ✓ **Campus Jobs:** the universities allow students to work on campus for up to 20 hours per week. These jobs often help the students recover their living expenses while studying at the university.

- ✓ **Summer Jobs:** each year, the student has two vacations totaling to three to four months. During this period, the student can work full time either on campus or off campus. International Students are not allowed to work off campus for the first nine months of their study. These jobs being full time in nature help the students make more money than what they require for their living expenses. Again, one has to be careful while selecting the university. You should apply to only those universities, which have on campus jobs are available.

If one uses the above information carefully while applying to the universities, the total cost of education, which requires funding through personal savings or educational loans comes down substantially.

This is one area in which Reaching UP has developed expertise through extensive research and experience. The students of Reaching UP therefore have saved thousands by applying to the right university, for the right program at the right time.

part six

Scholarships

6. Scholarships

Some US schools are more likely than others to offer financial aid for international undergraduate students. The lists below indicate which schools offer aid (including grants, loans, and jobs) to the largest numbers of international students.

To be included in the following lists, the schools must have an average award that is greater than 1/5 of the cost of attendance. The financial aid may include grants, and jobs, and often includes both merit and need-based awards. Within each group, schools are listed in alphabetical order.

If a school is not listed here, it probably does not have much financial aid for international students. However, it is worth noting that some schools may have athletic scholarships that are open to both international students and US students. The lists below do not count the number of athletic scholarships awarded to international students. In our course, www.rekindlemylife.com, we teach all about finding scholarships and teaching you how to master the process, giving you detail tools and resources to succeed.

Schools with Awards to More than 150 Students

Arizona State University (AZ)
Barry University (FL)
Clark Univ. (MA)
Eastern Michigan Univ. (MI)
Grinnell College (IA)
Harding Univ. (AR)
Harvard (MA)

Illinois Inst. of Tech. (IL)
Liberty Univ. (VA)
Louisiana State Univ. (LA)
Macalester College (MN)
Marquette Univ. (WI)
MIT (MA)
Mount Holyoke College (MA)

Ohio Wesleyan Univ. (OH)
Princeton (NJ)
Univ. of Bridgeport (CT)
Univ. of Houston (TX)
Univ. of Pennsylvania (PA)
Univ. of South Florida (FL)

Schools with Awards to 100-149 Students

Brown Univ. (RI)
Calvin College (MI)
College of Wooster (OH)
Dartmouth (NH)
Dordt College (IA)
Eckerd College (FL)
Florida Inst. of Tech. (FL)
Georgia Southern Univ. (GA)

Graceland College (IA)
Luther College (IA)
Middlebury College (VT)
Northeast Louisiana (LA)
Oberlin (OH)
Savannah Coll. of Art (GA)
Slippery Rock Univ. (PA)
Smith College (MA)

Stanford (CA)
Texas Christian Univ. (TX)
Tri-State Univ. (IN)

Univ. of Miami (FL)
Univ. of Rochester (NY)
Yale (CT)

Performance based scholarships

Some SELECT Universities in the USA offer merit-based scholarships each year to outstanding students. These scholarships are competitive and, unless otherwise indicated, are renewable for up to four years, provided you maintain good academic performance.

You may receive any combination of these scholarships up to an amount not to exceed the total cost of education plus $1,000. The total cost of education is determined annually by the Office of Financial Aid and includes tuition, fees, room and board, books and supplies, and personal and transportation expenses.

Need based scholarships

Again, only select universities, international students are welcome to apply for need-based financial aid. Along with university admission application, students should also submit International Student Financial Aid Application, Official letter from parent's employer stating gross income and value of prerequisites, subsidies, and/or benefits for the previous calendar year, Certification of Finances with a supporting bank letter.

Although a student applying for aid may be academically admissible, not all students will be awarded financial aid due to the limited availability of funding. In addition, all students receiving funds are expected to contribute personally toward educational and personal expenses while attending Villanova University.

International students are notified of financial aid eligibility at time of admission; those applying early will be notified of their financial aid eligibility earlier.

Recipients are required to re-apply for financial aid each year by submitting the College Board International Student Financial Aid Application and an updated official letter from parent's employer stating gross income and value of prerequisites, subsidies, and/or benefits.

Sports scholarships

Almost every university offers athletic scholarships according to the policies of the associations to which they belong. The types of scholarships that may be offered include archery scholarships, basketball scholarships, crew scholarships, cross country scholarships, field hockey scholarships, football scholarships, gymnastics scholarships, hockey scholarships, rifle scholarships, sailing scholarships, swimming scholarships, tennis scholarships, volleyball scholarships etc. Athletic scholarships are distributed in an equitable fashion among male and female students. Consequently, a considerable amount of financial aid is available for women with athletic ability.

Students should put together a profile of their athletic and academic qualifications. Include copies of the best newspaper clippings in which your performance is mentioned, letters of recommendation from your current coaches, and your sport's season schedule. A short 5-10 minute video of your athletic performance may also be helpful. Send copies of this athletic portfolio to the coaches at the schools you are interested in.

Most athletic scholarships provide only partial support, and require that the student maintain satisfactory academic grades for renewal. Coaches can also refuse to renew an athletic scholarship if the student's athletic performance falls short of expectations. If the student quits the team, the athletic scholarship is usually terminated. (Athletic scholarships are not terminated if the student is injured during competition.)

part seven

Entrance Test

7. Entrance Tests

Students from all over the world apply to American universities for admissions. They belong to different educational backgrounds and different grading systems. Many institutions have relied on the ACT or SAT as a grading test to determine the student aptitude. These are standardized test regulated by Non-governmental testing agencies. In order to compare their aptitude on a common platform, some universities in the United States require all the international students to take SAT (Scholastic Aptitude Test) for undergraduate studies, GRE (Graduate Record Examination) for graduate studies and GMAT (Graduate Management Admission Test) for MBA. Nearly every major university in America requires that the students take one of the above tests for admissions.

Similarly, in order to ensure that the student wanting to study in an American university is capable of understanding English, all universities in the United States require their applicants coming from non-native Englsih speaking countries to take TOEFL (Test of English as a Foreign Language).

So, if you want to study in USA after high school, you have to take SAT & TOEFL as two tests. If you want to go for your masters after graduation from college, you have to take GRE and TOEFL and if you are an MBA aspirant, you have to go for GMAT and TOEFL. These tests are conducted throughout the year. The scores of TOEFL are valid for two years; the scores of GMAT and GRE are valid for five years. Therefore, it is advisable to take these tests well before your applications to the American Universities.

GRE

The GRE General Test measures critical thinking, analytical writing, verbal reasoning, and quantitative reasoning skills that have been acquired over a long period of time and that are not related to any specific field of study.

Analytical Writing — The skills measured include the test taker's ability to

- articulate complex ideas clearly and effectively
- examine claims and accompanying evidence
- support ideas with relevant reasons and examples
- sustain a well-focused, coherent discussion
- control the elements of standard written English.

Verbal Reasoning — The skills measured include the test taker's ability to

- analyze and evaluate written material and synthesize information obtained from it
- analyze relationships among component parts of sentences
- recognize relationships between words and concepts.

Quantitative Reasoning — The skills measured include the test taker's ability to

- understand basic concepts of arithmetic, algebra, geometry, and data analysis
- reason quantitatively
- solve problems in a quantitative setting.

Who Takes It and Why?

Prospective graduate applicants take the General Test. GRE test scores are used by admissions or fellowship panels to supplement undergraduate records and other qualifications for graduate study. The scores provide common measures for comparing the qualifications of applicants and aid in evaluating grades and recommendations.

When and Where is it conducted?

The GRE Test is offered year-round at computer-based test centers. You can register for the test by logging on to www.gre.org and they will point you to the nearest testing center. It is always advantageous to register on time. Having a Pass port is necessary on the date of your test.

The GRE revised General Test places a **greater emphasis on higher-level cognitive skills**.

The overall testing time for the computer-based GRE revised General Test is about **3 hours and 45 minutes**, plus short breaks.

FEATURE OF NEW GRE:

- One Analytical Writing section with writing tasks of 30 minute each.

- New feature: Students can use an on-screen calculator.

- Two Verbal Reasoning sections & Two Quantitative Reasoning sections

- One unscored section, typically a Verbal Reasoning or Quantitative Reasoning section, which may appear at any point in the computer-based GRE revised General Test that **does not count** towards a score, may appear in any order.

- An identified research section that is **not scored** may also be included in the computer-based

GRE revised General Test will come at the end of the test.

- **A new test-taker friendly design** for the computer-based test: edit or change your answers, skip questions and more, all within a section. No more computer adaptability for every question is required.

The Analytical Writing section will always be first, while the other five sections may appear in any order.

Test structure and length of the computer-based test:

SECTION	NUMBER OF QUESTIONS	TIME
Analytical Writing (One section with two separately timed tasks)	One "Analyze an Issue" task and one "Analyze an Argument" task	30 minutes per task
Verbal Reasoning (Two sections)	Approximately 20 questions per section	30 minutes per section
Quantitative Reasoning (Two sections)	Approximately 20 questions per section	35 minutes per section
Unscored[+]	Varies	Varies
Research[++]	Varies	Varies
Table with breakdown of the timing and tasks for each test section		

You'll get a **10-minute break** following the third section and a **1-minute break** between the other test sections.

SCORE SCALE FOR THE REVISED GENERAL GRE TEST

- **Verbal Reasoning scores** will be reported on a new **130 – 170** score scale, in 1-point increments (versus 200 – 800 in 10-point increments).

- **Quantitative Reasoning scores** will be reported on a new **130 – 170** score scale, in 1-point increments (versus 200 – 800 in 10-point increments).

Analytical Writing scores will continue to be reported on the same **0 – 6** score level, in half-point increments.

SAT

The SAT tests students' reasoning based on knowledge and skills developed through their course work.

It measures their ability to analyze and solve problems by applying what they have learned in school.
The SAT Reasoning Test is a measure of the critical thinking skills you'll need for academic success in college. The SAT assesses how well you analyze and solve problems—skills you learned in school that you'll need in college.

The SAT has following three sections:

- Critical Reading
- Mathematics
- Writing

Each section of the SAT is scored on a scale of 200—800, with two writing sub-scores for multiple-choice and the essay.

The SAT includes a Critical Reading, Math, and Writing Section, with a specific number of questions related to content.

In addition, there is one 25-minute un-scored section, known as the variable or equating section. This un-scored section may be critical reading, math, or writing multiple-choice section. This un-scored section does not count toward the final score, but is used to try out new questions for future editions of the SAT and to ensure that scores on new editions of the SAT are comparable to scores on earlier editions of the test.

The 25-minute essay will always be the first section of the SAT, and the 10-minute multiple-choice writing section will always be the final section. The remaining six 25-minute sections can appear in any order, as can the two 20-minute sections. Test takers sitting next to each other in the same testing session may have test books with entirely different sections.

The SAT is developed and administered by the US-based "College Entrance Examination Board". This implies that Collegeboard sets the questions, conducts the test, and sends each examinee the score report.

SAT Subject Test:

Subject Tests measure your knowledge of particular subjects (literature, history, foreign languages, math, physics etc.) and your ability to apply that knowledge. Some of the U.S. colleges require or recommend one or more Subject Tests for admission or placement.

Colleges which don't require Subject Tests will still take them into consideration, since the tests offer a better picture of your academic abilities.

Subject Tests are also administered in the paper and pencil format. They contain multiple-choice questions and take one hour to complete.

Each test is scored on a scale of 200-800.

GMAT

The Graduate Management Admission Test® (GMAT®) is a standardized assessment that helps business schools assess the qualifications of applicants for advanced study in business and management. Schools use the test as one predictor of academic performance in an MBA program or in other graduate management programs.

What the GMAT Measures?

The GMAT exam measures basic verbal, mathematical, and analytical writing skills that you have developed over a long period of time in your education and work. It does NOT measure:

- your knowledge of business,
- your job skills,
- specific content in your undergraduate or first university course work,
- your abilities in any other specific subject area, or
- subjective qualities—such as motivation, creativity, and interpersonal skills.

Format and Timing

The GMAT® exam consists of three main parts, the Analytical Writing Assessment, the Quantitative section, and the Verbal section.

Analytical Writing Assessment

The GMAT® exam begins with the Analytical Writing Assessment (AWA). The AWA consists of two separate writing tasks—Analysis of an Issue and Analysis of an Argument. You are allowed 30 minutes to complete each one.

Quantitative Section

Following an optional ten-minute break, you begin the Quantitative Section of the GMAT exam. This section contains 37 multiple-choice questions of two question types—Data Sufficiency and Problem Solving. You will be allowed a maximum of 75 minutes to complete the entire section.

Verbal Section

After a second optional ten-minute break, you begin the Verbal Section of the GMAT® exam. This section contains 41 multiple choice questions of three question types—Reading Comprehension, Critical Reasoning, and Sentence Correction. You are allowed a maximum of 75 minutes to complete the entire section.

The purpose of the GMAT is to measure one's ability to think systematically and to employ the verbal and mathematical skills that one has acquired throughout his/her years of schooling.

The test does not aim to measure the knowledge of specific business or academic subjects. One is assumed to know basic algebra (but not calculus), geometry and arithmetic, to know the basic conventions of standard written English, and to be able to write an analytical essay.

Test-taking Strategies for GMAT
- Spend more time with the initial questions than the later questions.
- Answer as many questions as possible.
- Do an educated guess, if not sure with the answer.
- Pace yourself well and should be aware of remaining time.
- Confirm the answer only when he/she is confident about the selected option.
- Careful about section exit and test quit commands, as one cannot go back to the previous section

TOEFL

The Test of English as a Foreign Language (TOEFL) measures the ability of nonnative speakers of English to use and understand English as it is spoken, written, and heard in college and university settings. The TOEFL tests all four language skills that are important for effective communication: speaking, listening, reading, and writing. The test helps students demonstrate that they have the English skills needed for success. TOEFL also emphasizes integrated skills and provides better information to institutions about students' ability to communicate in an academic setting and their readiness for academic coursework.

The TOEFL test is developed and administered by the US-based "Educational Testing Service" (ETS). This implies that ETS sets the questions, conducts the test, and sends each examinee the test scores. For the conduct of the test, ETS has appointed Testing Agencies in various countries, which act as franchisee for ETS. Computer based TOEFL test is held all-round-the-year. Unlike other exams, you can choose your own date and time for taking the TOEFL test! You can register for the test at their websites.

Training at Reaching Up

Our courses are offered both as a home study and online with a learning environment designed to produce the best results. Reaching UP has been offering goal-driven and skill-enhancing courses and also the Scholarship Training Program our biggest success course to date. We have been a Value-leader for test training courses (GRE, GMAT, SAT, TOEFL etc…). We offer these courses that uniquely focus on real-time, student specific feedback to all students on their weaknesses.

www.rekindlemylife.com

The objective of our test preparation courses offered in online is to provide training with a view to imparting conceptual understanding of the test assessment areas. The objective of the training classes is also to arm students with efficient Procedures for dealing with the test sections, time-tested and 'works-every-time' Strategies for picking the correct answers to all Verbal and Quantitative problems, and unique Diagnostic support in all assessment areas so that each student can achieve a better score. We provide the best courses backed by the best score Guarantee.

SCORE GUARANTEE: Our entire test Courses are backed by our unique Score Improvement Guarantee, wherein you are guaranteed a test Score improvement of at least 20% to 80%. You will be required to validate the Score Guarantee by Completing to the best of your ability all of the mandatory Pre-Course assignments, by attending all the sessions of the training prep-class in which you are registered, by actively participating in the class tests and assignments, and by completing the post- course practice tests and exercises. You will also be required to take the test within 30 days of the last day of the final test.

part eight

Application Process

8. Application Process

The application process to a US Universities is a long and complicated affair. It involves extensive research on the internet, knowledge about the working method of American universities, accurate documentation and correct timing, to list just a few factors. In this chapter, we have given the various steps involved in the applications process.

Selection of Universities

Selecting universities is a very time consuming and important process not only from the admission point of view but also because applying to universities is very expensive by International student's standards. The application fee itself costs about seventy-five dollars ($75-US). Therefore, be very careful while applying to the universities.

The best university for you may not be the famous ones, but those that offer you your field of study as well as meet the other criteria important to you. The ranges of academic options as well as available universities are so wide that it is not possible to select the best in one go and it may take some time.

The basic steps involved in the process of selecting universities are

a) Decide on the field of education in line with your likings and past academic background

b) Assess your financial ability and budget

c) Now, select 20 to 30 universities based on the following criterion:

- ✓ Program Offerings
- ✓ Research programs
- ✓ University Rankings
- ✓ Program Length
- ✓ Cost—Tuition, living expenses etc
- ✓ Availability of Financial Assistance to International Students
- ✓ Entrance Requirements
- ✓ Tests (SAT, TOEFL etc and minimum scores)
- ✓ Accreditation status (Professional accreditation for some programs)
- ✓ Student Profile
- ✓ Enrollment—Total available seats and the size of the school
- ✓ Location (climate, semi-rural, metropolitan city etc)
- ✓ Facilities Library, housing, student associations etc.
- ✓ Type of Institution—Public or Private

These are the usual criteria. You could prioritize your criteria out of this list and shortlist the number of universities on that basis to about 10. You could further shortlist your choice on basis of specific issues like tuition fees, availability of financial etc.

Your past academic record is one of the most important deciding factors in getting admission to a college abroad. Most schools require you to have a reasonably academic record especially for technology and science programs and courses. Each university has its own minimum requirement for its programs, which are flexible depending on the candidate profile.

It is advisable not to convert your grades by your home country system but to the American Grade Point Average system since the conversion may not be accurate. You may attach an explanatory note from your college to indicate your rank in your class and/or university. The letter may also indicate your place as compared to the class and the university average and the number of students in the class and the number of colleges and students in the university. You may also provide any other information or documents that you feel may help you in the admission process.

Every university has its own minimum requirements and scores with respect to standardized tests. Check out the requirements of the universities and short-list the ones that will accept your scores.

Most international students are concerned about the high cost of education abroad and seek information on opportunities for financial assistance. The expenses for education abroad include tuition fees, living expenses, health insurance, transportation etc. This is an important criterion for selecting the courses as well as universities.

It is important to understand that most universities offer financial assistance to international students based primarily on merit and rarely on need. The amount, and type of assistance offered varies based on the university, department and level of study. Also funds are more likely to be available in fields like Engineering, Physical Sciences and Biological sciences.

Once you start receiving application forms and material, go through in detail for the various requirements and deadlines like the application deadline, minimum scores required in the standardized tests, recommendation letters needed and other such information.

Tabulate all these requirements and compare them with your objectives. Reaching UP can help you select universities that are best suited for your requirements.

Selection of Program

Selection of university and selection of program usually go hand in hand. But one must remember that even the best-known universities are not the best for every single program offered in that university. Similarly, a particular university may not be very high ranked, but a particular program in that university may be excellent for your requirements. Therefore, it is necessary to study each program very carefully.

Academic Documentation

Transcripts: students who are applying to American Universities would be required to submit a detailed report and transcripts (report cards) of all the years of higher studies in their home country. The transcripts form should be filled out by a college official like the principal, counselor or headmaster. This form should introduce you in the context of your whole school experience in relation to the other students in your class. Admission committees will be interested in learning how you have performed in your own educational system. The transcript should talk about your accomplishments and provide a prediction of your chances for success in university-level studies.

Since there is a variation between the styles of scoring used abroad and the ones used in your home country, ask your college to include a guide to the grading standards used in your educational system and your school. If your college ranks students by their level of academic achievement, make certain that the ranking is included with the other details. Also send the school / junior college leaving certificate as and when it is available. The transcripts must be in English only.

Recommendations: Letters of reference or recommendation letters play a very important part in your admission. A recommendation letter is a signed statement from a person who has taught you in a subject that is related to the course you are applying to. It should list your positive and negative qualities, strengths and other such information. The teacher must indicate his position, how long he/she has known the applicant and in what capacity. He/she should briefly discuss the need, importance and usefulness of the study the applicant proposes to undertake. Authors are usually asked to rank applicants in their letters of recommendation, which helps admission officers to interpret the academic credentials of foreign students. Students should obtain letters of recommendation from teachers who know them as a person as well as a student. You may like to request your author to give concrete examples that may show your qualities.

Statement of Purpose: The personal essays, and/or statement of purpose, play a very important role in the process of evaluating your application for both admission as well as financial aid because it gives the faculty assessing your application their most significant impression of you as an individual. This section is the key to distinguish your application from other suitable candidates and a chance to market yourself. A personal statement should include your reasons for choosing a particular course, the suitability of your education and experience for the chosen course, your personal interests and career goals. Some courses like Business school courses will have their own essay questions and format. Others may ask for a résumé or reasons for applying to that particular course.

Financial Documentation

You must submit a financial aid application if you desire financial help for your studies in a US university. Financial assistance for non-US citizens is very limited. The evidence of financial support is required by universities to issue the documents needed for visa application. Although it is a requirement for application, it is usually not taken into consideration into factors that determine admission. Most universities make their admission decisions without regard for the source and amount of financial support. This is why the course we teach in finding scholarships in US colleges is key and the information we provide at www.rekindlemylife.com is essential.

You would be required to submit documentation of your family's financial resources to help schools assess your need. Most of the universities have their own financial aid form, which you would have to complete. You would also be required to submit a bank statement demonstrating your financial capacity to support your education in US. Some US state institutions offer tuition waivers to international students in return for some type of educational contribution.

After applications:

Universities usually inform students of their admission decisions well in advance of the beginning term. If you have received admission in more than one university, you will have to decide which one you want to attend. At this

48

stage, you should compare a few objective and mostly more subjective criteria. The points you should focus on are program curriculum, length of program, choice of courses, funding offer or best program with respect to costs, Cost of living, Strength of related departments/program etc.

Once you have been accepted:

Each college will tell you exactly what steps to follow to confirm your acceptance of their offer of admission and how to prepare for your first term. This information will be included with the letter of admission or in materials that will be sent to you shortly thereafter. You must respond with a "Yes" or "No" for each offer of admission. You may also be required to submit a financial deposit to the institution that you plan to attend. This is to guarantee your place in the class. Make sure you do not miss any deadlines.

Admissions Counseling at Reaching UP

Reaching Up has guided lots of students through this process of applications. Accurate information and astute analysis are the key factors, which help students find a career and university of their choice at the same time our understanding of the funding issues has helped parents save thousands on the educational budget. We strongly recommend the students and parents to utilize our experience for their benefit. You can contact the counselor at our offices. This service is also available on line at www.rekindlemylife.com. We also provide this service through e mails and telephonic conversations to the students from all over the world.

part nine

VISA Issues

9. VISA Issues

This is the last and the most delicate of the steps while planning to study in the United States. Most students are scared and tensed by the time they reach this stage. But they need to understand that by being tense; they are increasing the chances of failure rather than reducing it. Instead, if they collect all the relevant information, make thorough preparation, and feel confident, there is nothing that can stop them from achieving their objective.

Requirements of students visa

What Visa Officers look for while issuing visa

A. Evidence of Residence Abroad: The consular officer may not issue a student visa unless satisfied that the applicant:

(1) Has a residence abroad ,

(2) Has no intention of abandoning that residence, and

(3) Intends to depart from the United States upon completion of the course of study.

Applicants generally establish their ties abroad by presenting evidence of economic, social, and/or family ties in their homeland sufficient to induce them to leave the United States upon the completion of studies.

How to Apply

All first time applicants of F-1 visa would need to make an appointment on the **US Consulate website in your country**. You have to take a hard copy (print-out) of the appointment made by you after the confirmation of the appointment. You can directly take the appointment page printout or if any mail that was sent to your mail by the

US Consulate. Without this printout of your appointment you will not be allowed to the interview.

VISA documentation

A. Consulate Documents:

a) DS-160 Confirmation Barcode printout

b) One photograph as per specification Photocopy of Form I-20 / DS2019. (whichever applicable)

c) Proof of payment of SEVIS Fee Receipt I-901, if applicable.

d) Photocopy of passport data pages (1st and last page).

e) Photocopy of the passport pages bearing "Observation" or "Remarks".

f) Original interview appointment letter.

g) Original, valid HDFC Bank visa fee receipt. (Embassy copy).

h) Dependent applicants must submit a photocopy of their respective I - 20 along with the principal applicant's I – 20.

i) Dependents must submit a photocopy of the principal applicant's visa

j) Visa renewal applicants must submit a copy of the previous expired U.S. visa stamped on their passport

B. US University Documents:

k) An I-20 Form, Please be sure to submit both pages of the I-20 form, signed by you and by a school official.

l) High School certificates or provisional certificates, grade reports, and transcripts from all previous institutions attended.

m) Scores from U.S. standardized tests such as the TOEFL, SAT/GRE/GMAT.

n) Financial evidence showing you have sufficient funds to cover your tuition and living expenses during the period of your intended study. You must demonstrate that funds are immediately available to cover the first year's costs, and show evidence that funds will be available for all subsequent years.

C. Proof of Funds Documents:
   a) Proof of ability to finance the education

   b) Scholarship letters,

   c) Bank letters,

   d) Salary slips of parents and other sponsors if any,

   e) Income Tax returns for last 2-3 years etc of parents and other sponsors if any.

   f) Rental receipts of own shops or buildings if any with revenue stamps.

   g) Sponsors Business P/L Account duly certified by a Certified (chartered) Accountant if sponsor is a businessman.

   h) Pension Papers - if sponsor is retired.

   i) 6 months of Bank records - i.e. Bank statements or Bank Passbooks of sponsors.

j) Affidavit of supports by sponsors and student separately.

k) Loan approval letters (if you want to show loans.)

VISA Interview

Try and gather information on the current trend, what the visa officer is expecting, why visa is being rejected, etc. Look for decisions and experiences particularly in the consulate where you will be appearing for the interview. Knowing what to expect helps!

When you go for the visa, dress well. Speak slowly and clearly. Don't appear tense and don't look desperate. Showing some self-confidence helps. They should never feel that you will have any sort of difficulty language, finance, racial, religious, etc.

Risk of VISA rejection

Yes. It is true that if your visa is rejected, all your efforts and money put into the process of studying in the United States go waste. But you can always apply for a second time and get your visa approved. As per the new rule, you can apply as many numbers of times as you want. (The application fee is to be paid every time). But the best way is to go well prepared right in the first time.

VISA Consultancy at Reaching Up

Reaching Up provides comprehensive visa documentation and interview training to its students. We are an international education consulting company. We have years of experience handling all type of student visas. We are specialists who handle only student visas and related matters. Our expertise lies in the fact that over the years we have handled all types of students with a very high success rate. Although ethically and by law, we cannot guarantee the outcome of any case, our rate of success is extremely high.

part ten

University Listing

10. University Listings

There is a trend amongst the students to blindly follow rankings while selecting the universities that they want to apply to. We have always given importance to the overall background of the university, the quality of a particular department and the academic and financial requirement of the student before selecting the university. The rankings can be used only as a guideline. We strongly believe that more often than not, a 29th ranked university may be much more appropriate for your career than the 17th ranked university. Therefore, take these rankings as a broad guideline and not a conclusive verdict about the standing of the university.

Top Engineering Schools

1   Massachusetts Inst. of Technology
2   Stanford University (CA)
    University of California–Berkeley *
4   California Institute of Technology
    U. of Illinois–Urbana-Champaign *
6   Georgia Institute of Technology *
    University of Michigan–Ann Arbor *
8   Carnegie Mellon University (PA)
    Cornell University (NY)
    Purdue Univ.–West Lafayette (IN)*
11 University of Texas–Austin *
12 Princeton University (NJ)
    Univ. of Wisconsin–Madison *
14 Johns Hopkins University (MD)
    Northwestern University (IL)
    Texas A&M Univ.–College Station *
    Virginia Tech *
18 Pennsylvania State U.–University Park *

Rensselaer Polytechnic Inst. (NY)
Rice University (TX)
Univ. of Minnesota–Twin Cities *
22 Duke University (NC)
Univ. of California–Los Angeles *
Univ. of California–San Diego *
Univ. of Maryland–College Park *
University of Washington *
27 Columbia University (NY)
Ohio State University–Columbus *
University of California–Davis *
University of Pennsylvania
31 Harvard University (MA)
North Carolina State U.–Raleigh *
University of Florida *
Univ. of Southern California
University of Virginia *
36 Brown University (RI)
Case Western Reserve Univ. (OH)
Iowa State University *
Univ. of California–Santa Barbara *
University of Colorado–Boulder *
41 Arizona State University *
Dartmouth College (NH)
Lehigh University (PA)
Michigan State University *
University of Notre Dame (IN)
Vanderbilt University (TN)
Washington University in St. Louis
Yale University (CT)
49 University of Arizona *
University of California–Irvine *
51 Colorado School of Mines *
Rutgers–New Brunswick (NJ)*
University of Delaware *
University of Iowa *

University of Missouri–Rolla *
Worcester Polytechnic Inst. (MA)
57 Clemson University (SC)*
Colorado State University *
Drexel University (PA)
Illinois Institute of Technology
Michigan Technological University *
Rochester Inst. of Technology (NY)
University at Buffalo–SUNY *
Univ. of Massachusetts–Amherst *
University of Pittsburgh *
University of Utah *
67 Auburn University (AL)*
Boston University
Northeastern University (MA)
Polytechnic University (NY)
SUNY–Stony Brook *
Syracuse University (NY)
Tufts University (MA)
University of Illinois–Chicago *
University of Tennessee *
Washington State University *
77 Brigham Young Univ.–Provo (UT)
Clarkson University (NY)
Kansas State University *
Oregon State University *
Tulane University (LA)
University of Connecticut *
University of Houston *
University of Kansas *
U. of North Carolina–Charlotte *
University of Rochester (NY)
87 New Jersey Inst. of Technology *
Oklahoma State University *
Southern Methodist University (TX)

Stevens Institute of Technology (NJ)
Texas Tech University *
Univ. of California–Riverside *
University of Cincinnati *
Univ. of Missouri–Columbia *
University of New Mexico *
University of Oklahoma *
97　CUNY–City College *
Louisiana State U.–Baton Rouge *
Univ. of California–Santa Cruz *
University of Kentucky *
Univ. of Nebraska–Lincoln *
102 George Washington University (DC)
Marquette University (WI)
New Mexico State University *
Ohio University *
San Diego State University *
SUNY–Binghamton *
University of Alabama *
University of Miami (FL)
University of Rhode Island *
Univ. of South Carolina–Columbia *
University of Texas–Arlington *
Univ. of Wisconsin–Milwaukee *
Utah State University *
Wayne State University (MI)*
West Virginia University *

* denotes a public school.

Top Management schools
1　University of Pennsylvania (Wharton)
2　Massachusetts Inst. of Technology (Sloan)
3　University of California–Berkeley (Haas) *
　　University of Michigan–Ann Arbor *
5　Carnegie Mellon University (PA)

New York University (Stern)
U. of North Carolina–Chapel Hill (Kenan-Flagler) *
University of Texas–Austin (McCombs) *
9   Univ. of Southern California (Marshall)
University of Virginia (McIntire) *
11 Indiana University–Bloomington (Kelley) *
12 Cornell University (NY)
Purdue Univ.–West Lafayette (Krannert) (IN)*
U. of Illinois–Urbana-Champaign *
Univ. of Minnesota–Twin Cities (Carlson) *
Univ. of Wisconsin–Madison *
Washington University in St. Louis (Olin)
18 Emory University (Goizueta) (GA)
Ohio State University–Columbus (Fisher) *
Pennsylvania State U.–University Park (Smeal) *
University of Arizona (Eller) *
22 Michigan State University (Broad) *
Univ. of Maryland–College Park (Smith) *
University of Notre Dame (IN)
University of Washington *
26 Arizona State University (Carey) *
Babson College (MA)
Georgetown University (McDonough) (DC)
University of Florida (Warrington) *
30 Boston College (Carroll)
Case Western Reserve Univ. (Weatherhead) (OH)
Texas A&M Univ.–College Station (Mays) *
University of Georgia (Terry) *
Wake Forest University (Calloway) (NC)
35 Brigham Young Univ.–Provo (Marriott) (UT)
Georgia Institute of Technology *
Southern Methodist University (Cox) (TX)
University of Colorado–Boulder *
University of Iowa (Tippie) *
40 Boston University

Syracuse University (Whitman) (NY)
Tulane University (Freeman) (LA)
University of Arkansas (Walton) *
University of Pittsburgh *
Univ. of South Carolina–Columbia (Moore) *
Virginia Tech (Pamplin) *

47 Bentley College (MA)
College of William and Mary (VA)*
CUNY–Baruch College (Zicklin) *
Florida State University *
George Washington University (DC)
Georgia State University (Robinson) *
Miami University–Oxford (Farmer) (OH)*
Univ. of Missouri–Columbia *
University of Oklahoma (Price) *
University of Tennessee *

57 Auburn University (AL)*
Rensselaer Polytechnic Inst. (Lally) (NY)
Santa Clara University (Leavey) (CA)
University of Alabama (Culverhouse) *
University of Kansas *
University of Kentucky (Gatton) *
Univ. of Nebraska–Lincoln *
University of Oregon (Lundquist) *
University of Utah (Eccles) *

66 Baylor University (Hankamer) (TX)
DePaul University (IL)
Louisiana State U.–Baton Rouge (Ourso) *
North Carolina State U.–Raleigh *
Northeastern University (MA)
Pepperdine University (Graziadio) (CA)
Rochester Inst. of Technology (NY)
United States Air Force Acad. (CO)*
University of Connecticut *
University of Illinois–Chicago *
Univ. of Massachusetts–Amherst (Isenberg) *

77 Clemson University (SC)*
   Iowa State University *
   Rutgers–New Brunswick (NJ)*
   San Diego State University *
   Temple University (Fox) (PA)*
   University at Buffalo–SUNY *
   Univ. of California–Riverside *
   University of Denver (Daniels)
   University of Miami (FL)
   University of Richmond (Robins) (VA)
87 American University (Kogod) (DC)
   Colorado State University *
   Fordham University (NY)
   Lehigh University (PA)
   Loyola University Chicago
   Marquette University (WI)
   Oklahoma State University *
   St. Louis University
   Texas Christian University (Neeley)
   Texas Tech University (Rawls) *
   University of Alabama–Birmingham *
   University of Delaware *
   University of Louisville (KY)*
   University of Mississippi *
   U. of North Carolina–Charlotte (Belk) *
   University of San Diego
   University of Texas–Dallas *
   Villanova University (PA)
   Washington State University *
106 George Mason University (VA)*
   James Madison University (VA)*
   Kansas State University *
   Loyola Marymount University (CA)
   University of Cincinnati *
   University of Houston (Bauer) *

University of Texas–Arlington *
Univ. of Wisconsin–Milwaukee *
Virginia Commonwealth University *
Washington and Lee University (VA)
116 Ball State University (IN)*
California State U.–Los Angeles *
Creighton University (NE)
Drexel University (LeBow) (PA)
Hofstra University (Zarb) (NY)
Northern Illinois University *
Ohio University *
Oregon State University *
Pace University (Lubin) (NY)
Rutgers–Newark (NJ)*
San Jose State University (CA)*
Seton Hall University (Stillman) (NJ)
Southern Illinois U.–Carbondale *
SUNY–Albany *
SUNY–Binghamton *
Trinity University (TX)
University of Central Florida *
Univ. of Colo.–Colorado Springs *
University of Dayton (OH)
University of Memphis (Fogelman) *
Univ. of Missouri–Kansas City (Bloch) *
University of New Mexico (Anderson) *
University of San Francisco (McLaren)
West Virginia University *
Wichita State University (Barton) (KS)*
141 Bowling Green State University (OH)*
Cal Poly–San Luis Obispo *
Florida International University *
Gonzaga University (WA)
John Carroll University (OH)
Kennesaw State University (Coles) (GA)*
Kent State University (OH)*

Loyola College in Maryland (Sellinger)
Loyola University New Orleans (Butt)
Mississippi State University *
Rutgers–Camden (NJ)*
Seattle University (Albers)
St. Joseph's University (Haub) (PA)
University of Alabama–Huntsville *
University of Colorado–Denver and Health Sciences Center *
Univ. of Missouri–St. Louis *
University of Nebraska–Omaha *
U. of North Carolina–Greensboro (Bryan) *
University of North Texas *
University of Rhode Island *
University of South Florida *
University of Tulsa (OK)
Xavier University (Williams) (OH)

* denotes a public school.

part eleven

Pre-Departure Information

11. Pre Departure Information

Travel Tips

1. After getting the visa the next thing to do is booking tickets.

2. Days before the flight, call the airline to confirm your reservation and to cross-check everything the travel agent may have told you.

3. Indicate the type of you wanted. This can be done at the time of booking the tickets with the travel agent.

4. Some airlines offer Frequent Flier programs implying that after a certain number of miles of flying with that airline you get a free ticket. Enroll in such programs.

5. Avoid transit of airline at airports a direct flight is the best. If change of airline can't be avoided, make sure that there is at least 4-6 hours gap between the scheduled arrival of one flight and the scheduled departure of the connecting flight.

6. Baggage is usually safe with a single airline while change of airline sometimes leads to misplaced luggage. Some airlines don't take care with baggage transfer. You may have to personally carry it (check this while booking)

7. Arrive at the airport at least 2 hours before the check-in time.

8. Drink lot of fluids on the flight. This will help you recover the jetlag very fast.

9. Many airlines are fussy about the weight of your carry-on baggage (hand luggage). It is always better to check with your travel agent regarding this.

10. Always keep a photocopy of your passport, tickets, and I-20. Contact info of your school in every baggage including your carryon baggage (hand luggage).

11. Always keep original copies of your Certified Accountant certificate, bank statements, sponsor's affidavit, passport, and admission letters in your carry-on baggage (hand-luggage). Sometimes, the immigration officer may ask you to present these at the airport.

12. Ideally, a student can bring $ 500/- in cash, $ 1000/- in travelers cheques and a personal draft of the amount equal to one semester's expenses. You may check your I-20 to determine this amount.

Things to be done in advance
1. Learn typing.
2. Learn driving (optional).
3. Learn to cook.
4. Make your passport valid for 6 months more than your stay indicated in your I-20
5. All other changes are best made in the U.S.
6. Make purchases (sweater, thermal underwear, winter coat)
7. Have a complete medical checkup done.
8. Get prescriptions & medicines for all common ailments
9. Get your eye-sight checked - get a new prescription. Buy at least one extra pair of glasses, lenses.
10. Get requisite immunization done (especially MMR). Fill in the Health and Immunization record form that has been sent to you with the I-20 packet.

Packing
1. Start your packing at least two days before departure date.

2. Buy two strong boxes - they should be able to withstand a lot of mishandling. They should be as large as possible within the size limitations (however most airlines are not very strict about baggage size).

3. Put identification marks and labels both inside & outside the boxes (apart from this, the airlines will also provide you with adhesive labels). Boxes with independent top & bottom are preferable.

4. Box specifications, as an example the Air India economy class baggage specifications to the USA are given below. Note the specifications may be different for other countries/airlines. 2 pieces of baggage with total linear dimension (l+b+h) not exceeding 270cm (106"). Moreover the total linear dimension of each piece should not be over 158cm (62").

5. The weight of each bag should not exceed 32kg (70lb).

6. Carry-on baggage: In addition you can carry a bag with linear dimension not exceeding 115cm (45") onboard (fits on overhead compartments).

7. For most other airlines the baggage specifications are similar. If you are taking a break outside USA/Canada contact your travel agent or airline for details.

Things to be kept in the boxes

1. Copy of all certificates/documents (originals in hand baggage).

2. Necessary books/notebooks (some suggested books are - Clark's Tables, a good dictionary/thesaurus, a booklet for unit conversion) [note: there should be no legal hassles taking photocopies of books - but don't flaunt them around campus.

3. Copy of address book/telephone book/diary.

66

4. Some stationery and related items suggested (not absolutely necessary - just for the first few weeks) are: Notepads, envelopes, file papers.

5. Medical history file.

6. Soap (bath), toothbrushes (slightly costly in the US).

7. You may want to bring audio cassettes, CDs of your favorite music.

8. You may want to enquire with the travel agent regarding valuable items on which custom duty may be levied.

9. All groceries, pickles and other food stuff MUST be sealed completely or they may be removed by the US customs.

Clothes

1. Usually clothes are machine washed once every two weeks hence two weeks supply of clothes is needed. Get all clothes little loose - clothes may shrink in machine wash or you might probably grow fat.

2. 14-15 sets of undergarments, 6-8 pair of socks, handkerchiefs.

3. Good swimming trunk, few shorts, T-shirts may be brought.

4. At least one tie, 1-2 belts.

5. Two ordinary towels.

6. One bed sheet, pajamas, thermal underwear (2-4), extra woolen sweater.

Don't worry yourself if you can't bring any of the items listed above most of them are available pretty cheap in the US

Things to be kept in Hand Baggage

1. I-20, passport, ticket, financial documents (CA certificate, Bank Statements), admission letter, affidavit of sponsor, all college or school mark sheets and related certificates.

2. First aid medicines. For example, tablets for headache, nausea, fever, loose motion.

3. Novel/magazines/books for in-flight reading, sweater. If you are coming in Fall, the weather will be hot enough, thus you would NOT need to wear any warm clothing then. Else you MUST be prepared to face extremely cold temperatures if you are arriving in Spring.

4. Address book/phone book (US)

5. Copies of your photo (passport size)

6. Things to survive for a week in case luggage gets misplaced (two sets of clothes, valuables like addresses etc.)

Things to be left at home

1. List of addresses/phone numbers at which info about you can be obtained.

2. One copy of all your important documents.

3. A copy of all relevant parts of Medical History files.

4. Arrange to collect/redirect mail from your room/hostel.

5. Arrange to apply/collect/mail your transcripts (about 10 in number preferable)

6. Your tailoring measurements.

7. Few blank signed papers - so that your parents can be authorized to look after anything on your behalf.

To do in the last week before the flight

1. Call up & find if there is any delay or change of schedule of the plane (inform the people coming to pick you up of any such change).

2. Rest well - ready to face the long journey / jet lag and bid bye to all concerned.

On the day of the flight, in-flight and later

1. As it is going to be a long flight wear something comfortable preferably cotton full hand shirt and trousers. Wear your shoes.

2. Be at the airport at least one hour before check in time.

3. Relax during flight, sleep as much as possible.

4. For vegetarians, watch out before you eat for you may get non-vegetarian food even if you had asked for vegetarian. Veg. food is generally bland - fruits/juice are good choices.

5. Never hesitate to ask questions.

6. Once out of your home country be very careful (from sheer experience of seniors). Don't trust anyone. Don't hire a taxi (unless emergency) till you reach your destination. If required don't hesitate to spend money.

7. Don't hesitate to talk to people to ask questions. Usually people will answer all your queries satisfactorily.

Port of entry procedures

1. Sometime before landing the flight attendant will distribute customs declaration forms & immigration forms as mentioned below. Fill these out on the plane (you will submit them to the appropriate authorities when you land). Do not hesitate to take the flight attendant's help.

www.rekindlemylife.com

2. You can indicate that you have nothing to declare & total value of all goods you carry is less than $100 on the customs form.

3. Fill form I-94 in the plane. After seeing your documents, immigration officer will indicate length of stay, university, etc. This will be attached to your passport. You must retain this I-94 form; else you will face trouble in leaving USA later.

4. Form I-20 ID copy - all transactions regarding your non-immigrant status will be recorded in this form. This should be retained at all times (not surrendered when you temporarily leave the US). Your admission number will be given - memorize it & note it elsewhere.

5. Just before you land the correct local time will be announced set your watch [dual time watch will come in handy here]

6. Once you are out of the plane go straight to the immigration counter. It might take half to one hour here.

7. Keep your I-20, passport, admission & aid letters ready. They might ask few questions like - is this your first time in the US? -Are you a student on F1 visa? -Which University are you joining?

8. The immigration officer will attach an I-94 card on one of the pages of your passport usually against the visa page.

9. Be very relaxed and answer all the questions that the officer will ask. Sometimes the officer may ask you to present financial documents or letters from your sponsors. Thus it is advisable to carry these along with you in your carryon baggage (hand-luggage).

10. Then go to the conveyor belts to collect your luggage. Pick up a cart to carry the bags. Then pick up your bags as

they come out on the conveyor (suitable eye-catching labels help here). If you don't get your baggage inform the enquiry section.

11. Cart your baggage to nearby Customs. If asked, tell the officer that you are a student on F-1 visa, school, department and coming to USA for the first time. If asked to open the baggage, do so slowly but do not mess up the place. Note: In most cases you will NOT be asked to open your boxes at all & will be simply waved through.

12. Never leave your baggage unattended. Don't go out of the airport until somebody comes to receive you. If you have doubt the person who has come to receive you, don't hesitate to ask for his/her identification.

13. Once you reach your house (or other destination) call home & inform them of reaching safely.

part twelve

Dream Changers

12. Dream changes

Many a times, we are asked how can we work with so much intensity and still don't burn out. The answer to this question can be found in the following feed backs that our students have given. If we can be a source of inspiration and happiness of this high quality to so many students, we can do our work with so much intensity for many more years!

Michael Kwashi

"You can call Mr. Nigel at 11:00 in the night if you have a question" That is to show the kind of dedication you can get from him and his team. I was nervous before the interview at the embassy and as a native of Ghana, I was wondering. You see, I was surprise who all the information I was given was so easy and I was able to follow the process. Mr. Nigel was always ensuring I followed the plan, we set out for me and in 8 months, I was able to pass the GRE and get a scholarship to attend University of Buffalo for a Masters in Engineering. I could not have made this without the Reaching Up Team. From the test preparation, Visa Interview sample and walk through and Departure planning. I was supported all the way. This is something I never know existed and with a merit scholarship too made it a dream come through.

Basdeo Jailal

When I first learn of Reaching Up, I was wondering if it was real. My cousin told me that Mr. Nigel will help me, I was very hesitant since I was disappointed before by another agency. He is a person who will not only solve your education related queries, but also guide you at personal level. The comfort level he shares with his Students is really amazing. I had my online classes for the SAT, we went through all the preparations and I was happy to get great scores. Today, I am in Washington DC studying for my B.Sc. and I wanted to be a medical doctor one day, but with my not paying for my education, I was able to get a full scholarship. I want to thank Mr. Nigel Williamson and this Reaching Up people for making this possible for me. I told my aunt and cousins to start using him too as they are preparing to do their masters.

Noah Dewitt

With all the internet scams I hear about, I taught this was another one. I lost money before and since I finish my college two years before, I wanted more school in USA. Mr. Nigel had my grades on the computer and we decide to work on my English, work on my test score and writing. Then we start sending scholarships application to many organizations. I prepare for the GMAT and TOEFL and every week, I had on internet class with Reaching UP. They help me and my scores were high. I am happy to know others are teaching me and my applications for scholarship came back with approval. Not only that, I got accepted to 4 universities but I took the one with more scholarship money. I only have to pay room and board. Thanks for all the help from Mr. Nigel and the Reaching Up TV show.

Absheki Devi,

Thank you so much Mr. Nigel for your show and for your online program. I was able to find a scholarship and accepted to University of Maryland. The Visa preparation was great and I was nervous but you help me to stay calm. Reaching Up staffs are really nice people and I will always be grateful for how you help us. Although we did not know where I was gonna get the money from to pay for college, you work with me and all the scholarship applications and university application until I was accepted. Thanks very much. I will always be grateful for what you do for Jamaican people.

The most important thing is Mr. Nigel 24/7 availability Believe me I have received his e-mails at 1.30am, such is the dedication of this person.

Today there are three admits in my hand, my VISA approved, & this entire credit goes to Mr. Nigel & his wonderful team called Reaching Up.

part thirteen

In Closing

13. In Closing…

If you have reached up to this point by reading all the material in the previous chapters, you might have realized that the option of studying in the USA is extremely advantageous, affordable and practical. What you require is accurate guidance and a need of a friend, companion and guide in the whole process.

This is the precise role played by Reaching Up for the last 5 years. With the Internet, the world has come much closer. This is the time when the geography has become history. More and more parents are willing to send their children to the land of opportunities. The liberalized policy of the governments towards international mobility of students, increasingly affordable educational loans from the banks and the generous amount of funding available at the right American universities for the right students has made all the difference.

However, before making the final decision, it is always a good idea to collect as much as information as possible. What is more important is to analyze this information efficiently to help you in taking a well-informed decision. Reaching UP will be glad to help you in this regard. You can visit us at www.rekindlemylife.com

In Learning the Secrets to become an International Student, Nigel Williamson explores and identifies the specifics things you need to succeed at becoming an International Student in the US. This book would not tell you things you might do but it tells you exactly what to do and how to do it. Drawing on his wealth of experience both as an educator and consultant Nigel shares with you the key in becoming a good thinker and succeed as a student in the US.

Good thinkers are always in demand. A person who knows how may always get a job but the person who knows why will always be his boss. It's hard to overstate the value of changing your thinking. Good thinking can do many things for you generate revenue, solve problems and create opportunities. It can take you to a whole new level – personally and professionally. It really can change your life.

"This is an important book, very actionable and easy to follow steps leading to exciting opportunities and possibilities as an international student."

John Morales, Managing Partner, Ebine Estates

"Nothing like this has ever existed when I was trying to come to the US. It will spear you all that pain and frustration. I love the depth that Nigel Williamson goes into. This is so complete. True must read for International Students."

Ghabira, International Student, Kenya

" A road map to any student who wants to come to the US. Greatly needed Message!"
Dr. Steven Strein, International Student Advisor, Middle States College.

Nigel G. Williamson

Discover the Secrets of Winning Scholarships as an International Student at US Colleges

flavors
of hope